ENCOUNTERS IN

YOGA
AND
ZEN

Trevor Leggett

# ENCOUNTERS IN

## Meetings of Cloth and Stone

Charles E. Tuttle Company
Rutland, Vermont & Tokyo, Japan

# AND ZEN

Published by the Charles E. Tuttle Company, Inc.
of Rutland, Vermont & Tokyo, Japan
with editorial offices at
2-6 Suido 1-chome, Bunkyo-ku, Tokyo 112
First published by Routledge & Kegan Paul Ltd.

© 1993 by Charles E. Tuttle Publishing Co., Inc.

First Tuttle edition, 1993


LCC Card No. 82-15131
ISBN 0-8048-1909-2

Printed in Japan

# DEDICATION

To the late Hari Prasad Shastri,
in whom the ancient traditions were always young,
this collection of pieces is reverently dedicated.

# CONTENTS

# PREFACE

Stories of the type presented here are used in many spiritual schools, to a greater or lesser extent; nearly all teachers make some use of them. I have collected these over the years from a variety of sources: sometimes reminiscences of a former teacher are buried in an old book, or a temple magazine; one or two are folk stories, some are verbally transmitted, some would be difficult to trace to a source. There are one or two incidents personally experienced, and I have occasionally put a few introductory remarks.

Their function is to act as flint and steel in making a light. In this, the flint is gripped in the left hand, with some dry tinder (usually a herb) under the thumb near the edge; then the steel is struck with a glancing blow across the edge of the flint. There may be no spark; then one tries again. There may be a spark which does not touch the tinder; then one tries again. But when a spark does set the tinder smouldering, as must happen sooner or later, it has to be carefully blown on – not too much and not too little – till it glows brightly. Finally a spill of thin paper can be ignited, and that in turn lights the lamp or fire.

If a story here strikes no spark, or if there is a spark which dies away so that it does not recur in the mind, then another can be tried. When one does grip the mind, it should be pondered daily for several weeks, to find the deeper points. At the end of the introduction an example is given of how to focus on one such point. The process corresponds to nurturing the little glow of the tinder; it should not yet be subjected to the strong wind of outside criticism or scepticism or even constructive suggestion. It must be cherished inwardly. If all goes well and it creates a blaze, then outer winds, however strong, can only increase it.

These stories are not the same as Zen koans, in many of which something apparently extraordinarily inappropriate is said, or perhaps done; just because these are extraordinary, they are good for

# PREFACE

catching the mind. But afterwards the light from them has to be applied to daily life. The pieces presented here are often incidents from ordinary life (not that there are no extraordinary ones too). The aim is to find realization and inspiration from daily life. Because they are ordinary, it may be harder to focus upon them; but the traditional presentation is skilful at catching at the heart of an attentive reader.

In the Jewish tradition, Jesus was the first person known to have made systematic use of the method of riddle. He never spoke to the people except in riddles, says the Gospel. He expected these to be solved: to disciples asking for an explanation he replied briefly, 'Are you as dull as the rest?' (Interested readers may find a stimulus in the Buddhist priest's comment on pearls and swine, page 44.) His use of the riddles was itself one, echoing and extending the riddle in Isaiah: 'to those outside everything comes by way of riddles, so that (as Scripture says) they may look and look, but see nothing; they may hear and hear, but understand nothing; otherwise they might turn to God and be forgiven.'

# THE PICTURES

The pictures were brushed for this book by Jacques Allais in what is called the Suiboku style, in which he is an expert. His work has been praised by the doyen of Japanese Suiboku painters, Nanpu Katayama, who received the Order of Culture (corresponding to the British Order of Merit) for his services to art.

Suiboku is eighty per cent suggestion – a Suiboku artist would not show both ends of a bridge, only one. The style gives a hint for the focusing of meditation practice.

I am grateful to Jacques Allais for his generosity in offering these pictures for the book.

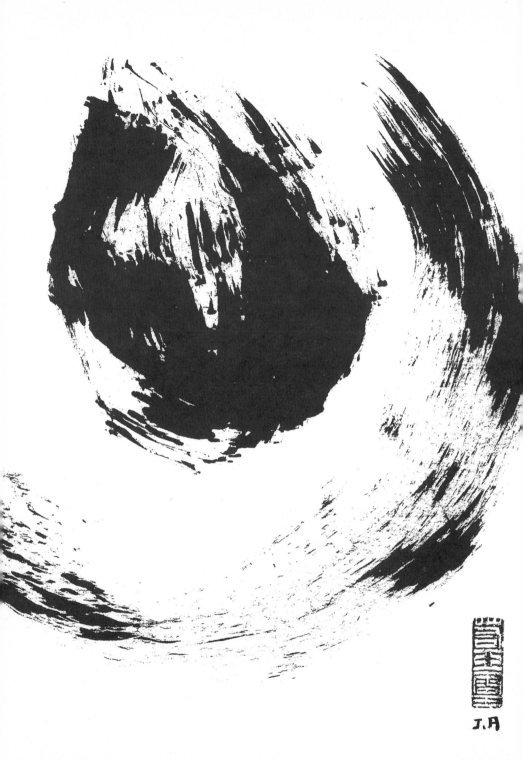

# INTRODUCTION

> Cloth against cloth, or stone against stone:
>> No clear result, and it is meaningless.
> Catch the flung stone in the cloth,
>> Pin the wind-fluttered cloth with a stone.

This verse comes in a scroll of spiritual training belonging to one of the knightly arts in the Far East. In these traditions, instruction is given in the form of vivid images, not in terms of logical categories; it is meant to be a stimulus to living inspiration, not dead analysis. The apparent exactitudes of logic turn out to be of very limited value when applied to life, because then the terms can never be precisely defined.

In the verse, the catching cloth stands for what is technically called 'softness', which is not the same as weakness; the stone stands for hardness, not the same as strength.

Softness has a special meaning: it is not merely giving way or doing nothing. There is a strength in softness, but it is not the hard strength of rigidity which has an inherent weakness, namely incapacity to adapt. There is another verse which illustrates these distinctions:

> Strong in their softness are the sprays of wisteria creeper,
> The pine in its hardness is broken by the weak snow.

How do these things work in practice? Here is an example from one of the schools of self-defence. You stand on the edge of a cliff and suddenly you see a powerfully built man rushing at you with outstretched arms to push you off. However you may brace yourself, the impetus of his rush will overcome your resistance, and after a brief check you will inevitably go over. To brace yourself is hardness, and it loses to greater hardness. This is meeting stone with stone. Yet if you do nothing, but just stand there – weakness – he will easily push you over.

# INTRODUCTION

Now suppose that just before his arms touch you, you fall in a heap at his feet. His impetus, not meeting the expected resistance, carries him on unopposed; he trips over you, and goes over himself. This is softness and it defeats hardness. Softness is controlled, skilfully directed, inwardly calm, and prompt. To rate as true softness, it has to be effective in application.

Softness must be carefully distinguished from weakness. In the second verse, the snow falls on the wisteria creeper. When it piles up a little, the flexible creeper bends and the snow drops off. It should be noted that the creeper does not give up its root. It retains an inner integrity, but is able to give before the external pressure by changing its posture, so to say. The branches of the pine tree, however, stiffly retaining their fixed attitude, hold the snow as it piles up, and they may be broken. (The fact is sometimes a surprise to those who have never seen it happen.)

Hardness too has a role. but it has to be used skilfully, just so much and no more. 'Pin the wind-fluttered cloth with a stone': the cloth unguided by human hands stands for weakness, and then the hardness of the stone is needed to hold it steady against the wind.

What is the application in life? 'Cloth against cloth, stone against stone: no clear result, and it is meaningless.' The sense is, not to meet weakness with weakness, nor oppose hardness with further hardness.

Do not meet cloth with cloth. They are those who, when they become aware of some undesirable characteristic in themselves which hampers their development, say with lethargic resignation, 'Well, that is how I am.' Sometimes they say, 'That is how God made me – it is His will.' This is meeting weakness with further weakness, and as the verse says, there is no result and it is meaningless.

Some IQ tests have shown Chinese and Japanese children as the best in the world at them. If it is accepted that to solve such little brain-teasers is important for life, the answer for the rest of us is to

3

# INTRODUCTION

work harder. The weakness, if it exists, is not to be indignantly denied or resented, but overcome by controlled and skilful hardness. Many great champions in sport began with an inferior natural endowment; they took it as a challenge, and finally surpassed the 'naturals', most of whom get their successes too early, become complacent and do not practise enough. Maria Callas did not have a first-rate natural voice: she trained a second-rate instrument. But the intensity of training gave her performances a magnetism which great natural singers have often lacked, and her impact on the world of music was enormous. Michelangelo was early on producing juvenile masterpieces, but the works attributed to Leonardo's youth do not foreshadow the genius that was to come; he drew it forth out of himself by persistent endeavour – 'ostinato rigore' as he says in his notebooks.

The hardness of the stone of will is absolutely necessary to pin the mind-cloth, fluttered by a wind of feeling of inherent limitation. The experience of spiritual teachers is that there are almost infinite potentialities in the mind of each man, which can be unfolded by faith and persistent application.

Again, when the gale of desire, whipped up by conventional acceptance – 'everyone is doing it' – tries to bear away all self-control, reasonings and counter-persuasions are often helpless; the stone of will to follow tradition must be used to hold it steady. Observation, too, shows how a released cloth, riding on the wind, seems at first free and glorious in its flight, but rain comes, and the sky-borne cloth begins to fall. It catches on a bramble. Now when the wind blows more, it is torn. Finally it always ends up, sodden with slime, in a ditch. The cloth that has been pinned by a stone is not carried away; it remains clean and useful, perhaps to fulfil itself one day by washing the face and hands of a bodhisattva.

Whether it is an inner wind or an outer wind that blows, the cloth of mind has to be held firm by the stone of will. Do not meet cloth with cloth.

# INTRODUCTION

Now the other case: do not meet stone with stone. Take the first story in this book. A young boy loses his father and finally enters a training monastery to try for spiritual realization. An elder pupil resents his keenness, persecutes him, and one day hits him hard on the arm with iron tongs. As it happens, this comes to the notice of the abbot. What is to be done? This is, so to say, a stone flung at the very heart of the young aspirant: a spiritual training centre, and then an actual physical attack by another pupil.

One way would be for the teacher to transfer the boy to another temple for a time, until the elder pupil had finished the obligatory three years training and left. That would be meeting the situation, the flung stone, with weakness. It does not catch the stone at all, but runs away.

Another solution would be to say, 'You must simply endure this. All the spiritual heroes of the past have endured such persecutions.' The teacher speaks from the heights: 'Sit here beside me and let us meditate on endurance.' This meets hardness with hardness, stone with stone. It can work, but it is liable to produce a hard character.

What other method is there? How is the stone of persecution to be caught in the cloth? How is softness to be applied here? One answer is given in the story on page 19. The teacher finds a means to come down from the mountain-top, and really sit beside the pupil in his distress.

Reading a story like one of these, the usual course is to come to the end and think, 'Ah yes, yes indeed', and then move on. It passes out of mind and is not recalled. But a real seeker will find that some particular one may keep recurring to him. That is a sign that it has something for him which he has not fully realized, and then it has to be read in a different way – slowly, sentence by sentence and ultimately word by word. If not too long, it is best to learn it by heart. A deeper point must be sought in it, and a still further one beyond that.

# INTRODUCTION

As an example, here is a story which first appeared in my *First Zen Reader*, and which has found its way into some anthologies. I have sometimes heard it discussed, and it was clear that some who liked it had not thought of going further into it. So they missed half the point. Here it is:

A young man who had a bitter disappointment in life went to a remote monastery and said to the abbot: 'I am disillusioned with life and wish to attain enlightenment to be freed from these sufferings. But I have no capacity for sticking long at anything. I could never do long years of meditation and study and austerity; I should relapse and be drawn back to the world again, painful though I know it to be. Is there any short way for people like me?' 'There is,' said the abbot, 'if you are really determined. Tell me, what have you studied, what have you concentrated on most in your life?' 'Why nothing really. We were rich, and I did not have to work. I suppose the thing I was really interested in was chess. I spent most of my time at that.'

The abbot thought for a moment, and then said to his attendant: 'Call such-and-such a monk, and tell him to bring a chessboard and men.' The monk came with the board and the abbot set up the men. He sent for a sword and showed it to the two. 'O monk,' he said, 'you have vowed obedience to me as your abbot, and now I require it of you. You will play a game of chess with this youth, and if you lose I shall cut off your head with this sword. But I promise that you will be reborn in paradise. If you win, I shall cut off the head of this man; chess is the only thing he has ever tried hard at, and if he loses he deserves to lose his head also.' They looked at the abbot's face and saw that he meant it: he would cut off the head of the loser.

They began to play. With the opening moves the youth felt

# INTRODUCTION

the sweat trickling down to his heels as he played for his life. The chessboard became the whole world; he was entirely concentrated on it. At first he had somewhat the worst of it, but then the other made an inferior move and he seized his chance to launch a strong attack. As his opponent's position crumbled, he looked covertly at him. He saw a face of intelligence and sincerity, worn with years of austerity and effort. He thought of his own worthless life, and a wave of compassion came over him. He deliberately made a blunder and then another blunder, ruining his position and leaving himself defenceless.

The abbot suddenly leant forward and upset the board. The two contestants sat stupefied. 'There is no winner and no loser,' said the abbot slowly, 'there is no head to fall here. Only two things are required,' and he turned to the young man, 'complete concentration, and compassion. You have today learnt them both. You were completely concentrated on the game, but then in that concentration you could feel compassion and sacrifice your life for it. Now stay here a few months and pursue our training in this spirit and your enlightenment is sure.' He did so and got it.

One of the things in the story that is not clear to most readers – in fact it never occurs to them – is this: the man had been rich, but had never bothered to use his money to relieve the sufferings of the poor, whom he must have seen often. He spent all his time on a trivial amusement. Where did the wave of compassion come from? He had not felt it before. A time when one's own life is in danger is the least likely occasion for a sudden feeling of compassion. Even in law, if two men are drowning in the sea and there is a tiny raft which will support only one, it is not murder, or any crime at all, to push off the other and leave him to drown. It is permissible in order to save one's

# INTRODUCTION

own life. So how is it that the hero suddenly felt compassion, and
became truly heroic? It is only one of the deeper points, but a very
important one.

The story first appeared over twenty years ago, and has, I imagine,
now shot its bolt, so it may be allowable to use it as an example to
illustrate the method of focusing on a point. However it is against
tradition to give more than a hint. I propose simply to set out the text in
a special way, which will, to those interested, provide that hint.

A young man who had a bitter disappointment in life went to a remote monastery and said to the abbot: 'I am disillusioned with life and wish to attain enlightenment to be freed from these sufferings. But I have no capacity for sticking long at anything. I could never do long years of meditation and study and austerity; I should relapse and be drawn back to the world again, painful though I know it to be. Is there any short way for people like me?' 'There is,' said the abbot 'if you are really determined. Tell me, what have you studied, what have you concentrated on most in your life?' 'Why, nothing really. We were rich, and I did not have to work. I suppose the thing I was really interested in was chess. I spent most of my time at that.'

The abbot thought for a moment, and then said to his attendant: 'Call such-and-such a monk, and tell him to bring a chessboard and men.' The monk came with the board and the abbot set up the men. He sent for a sword and showed it to the two. 'O monk,' he said, 'you have vowed obedience to me as your abbot, and now I require it of you. You will play a game of chess with this youth, and if you lose I shall cut off your head with this sword. But I promise that you will be reborn in paradise. If you win, I shall cut off the head of this man; chess is the only thing he has ever tried hard at, and if he loses he deserves to lose his head also.' They looked at the abbot's face and saw that he meant it: he would cut off the head of the loser.

They began to play. With the opening moves the youth felt the sweat trickling down to his heels as he played for his life. The chessboard became the whole world; he was entirely concentrated on it.

At first he had somewhat the worst of it,

but then the other made an inferior move

and he seized his chance to launch a strong attack.

As his opponent's position tumbled, he looked covertly at him. He saw a face of intelligence and sincerity, worn with years of austerity and effort. He thought of his own worthless life, and a wave of compassion came over him.

He deliberately made a blunder

and then another blunder, ruining his position and leaving himself defenceless.

The abbot suddenly leant forward and upset the board. The two contestants sat stupefied. 'There is no winner and no loser,' said the abbot slowly, 'there is no head to fall here. Only two things are required,' and he turned to the young man, 'complete concentration, and compassion. You have today learnt them both. You were completely concentrated on the game, but then in that concentration you could feel compassion and sacrifice your life for it. Now stay here a few months and pursue our training in this spirit and your enlightenment is sure.' He did so and got it.

# IRON RODS

A boy of twelve in Japan lost his father, to whom he was much attached. The shock and desolation turned his mind to Buddhism, and he asked his uncle, now looking after the family and himself a devout Buddhist, whether he could enter a temple. The uncle believed that the change in the heart was permanent, and took him to a training temple where the famous teacher accepted him.

The boy was very keen, and when the uncle made one of his monthly visits to see how he was getting on, the teacher remarked, 'He is trying with everything he has: he is making good progress.'

In this temple there happened to be at the time a monk of about nineteen, whose family owned a rich temple, for which he was destined to become the priest for life. As can happen, his initial interest in Buddhism had become secondary to his anticipation of the easy life he would have once he got through the four or five years of the training. Naturally he did not like the assiduous studying and service of the little boy, because it reminded him obscurely of what he himself might have done. One day in the winter he shouted to him to bring some water for the kettle. In a traditional temple this hung on a big chain above the charcoal fire, which is stoked by means of a pair of iron rods, rather like long chop-sticks.

As the boy was putting the water down he was shouted at again, and gave a start which spilled a little of the water. 'Clumsy idiot!' yelled the senior boy, and picking up the iron rods, hit him hard on the arm just above the wrist. Perhaps he hit harder than intended, or perhaps not, but in any case it was quite a severe blow. The small boy kept back his tears till he was dismissed, but then rushed out of the temple into a bamboo grove to cry.

It so happened that the uncle was making his visit that day, and he saw his nephew running into the trees. He went quickly after him and asked, 'What's happened – why are you crying?'

'It's nothing.'

# IRON RODS

'No, it's something. And what's that on your arm?' An ugly mark was beginning to come up.

'Oh, I knocked it.'

'That's not the mark of a knock. Someone's hit you.'

He dragged the boy with him into the temple and pushed in to see the teacher. 'Look at this! He's been hit, and you said yourself that he was keen and trying his very best. This is supposed to be a centre of spiritual training, and look what happens!'

The teacher got up and fetched a book of sermons of the Buddha, found a particular place, and handed it to the boy saying, 'Read from here.' The uncle sat fuming while his nephew read in a choked voice. When the sentence came: 'One who practises endurance will be a spiritual hero', the teacher said, 'Read that sentence again slowly, and we'll meditate on it together.'

The uncle shouted, 'It's easy to meditate when you haven't been hit!'

'Yes,' said the teacher, 'it's easier to meditate when you haven't been hit.'

He picked up the iron rods from the charcoal fire in his own room, and hit with all his force on his own arm. 'Now,' he said gently, 'let's meditate together: One who practises endurance will be a spiritual hero.'

# THE PREACHER

A famous preacher of Vedanta had a pupil of sixteen years who, under his instruction, acquired a very fine knowledge of the philosophy. He did not teach him rhetoric, as he did not consider that the boy would make a good speaker.

One day however the master suddenly became ill just before he had to address a gathering. On an impulse, he sent the boy to speak in his place, telling him to explain the circumstances, and then try to give a plain exposition of the fundamentals, as he had been taught.

To his surprise, it was reported to him that the speech by his pupil had been a great success. A little later, kindly friends hinted that it had even been said that the pupil was a better speaker than his master. ('Absurd, of course, but we felt you ought to know.')

The preacher pondered for a little while, and then set the pupil to re-make the garden of the house and build a shed in it, telling him that he should know about ordinary life as the layman lived it, and not only about abstractions. On another occasion when the master was again ill, he simply sent an excuse by the hand of the boy, who passed it on and returned at once.

After three months of this, the preacher noticed that his pupil, who had seemed rather downcast, had recovered his serenity and cheerfulness.

'It has been a test for him,' he confided to a close friend, a man of spiritual discernment. 'He must have been very disappointed, but he has overcome that now. He has done well in this test.'

'And how do you think you have done?' asked the friend.

# THE WINE POT

The final word of Mahayana Buddhism, as expressed in the Garland Sutra of China, is that Samsara, this world of suffering, is Nirvana, and the passions are enlightenment, bodhi. It is only illusion that causes us to see differences between them. 'Samsara *is* Nirvana, the passions *are* enlightenment.' This formula has sometimes been taken as a sort of slogan, in isolation from the spirituality of the rest of the Sutra, like the remark of St Paul, 'To the pure, all things are pure.'

A man who set himself up as a Buddhist teacher began preaching the slogan that passions are enlightenment, claiming to exemplify it by himself drinking heavily and frequenting brothels.

This was reported to a real saint who remarked briefly, 'No one who is a slave to passions can claim to see them as enlightenment.'

The teacher came storming round to the home of the saint and shouted, 'You people claim to teach the doctrine that Samsara is Nirvana and the passions are enlightenment, but you are afraid to live it. You cower behind the little wall of your petty prohibitions and commandments. "Do this, don't do that!" all the time. By giving all these silly rules, you are denying what you teach. Now I actually *live* it; perhaps you can see my life as passions, but I see it as enlightenment, following the flow of change which is the Buddha-nature. That's the difference between us. I am a real teacher because I live it; you are not, because you don't.'

The saint said, 'This kind of teaching will be of no use to the people.'

'Why not, why not?' cried the teacher.

'We won't argue about it,' the saint told him, 'but there is something else. We don't drink here, but we do keep some wine for guests who may come. Now some time back I was given a little of a very rare wine – would you like to give me your opinion of it?'

'Why yes, yes!'

The saint went out to give instructions to his attendant; as he came

# THE WINE POT

back into the room he turned his head and called back, 'Absolutely clean, mind!'

When the wine came, the guest could smell the delicious fragrance of it. But to his amazement, it was served to him in what would correspond in the West to an old chipped chamber-pot.

'What's this?' he cried.

'Oh, don't mind that. It's absolutely clean, I assure you – absolutely. What does it matter what the wine is served in? It's a very rare wine, they say.'

The guest tried to drink, but found he could not. He put the chamber-pot down and said quietly, 'Why are you doing this?'

The saint replied, 'This vessel has been specially made absolutely clean, and the wine is a choice one. But you cannot drink it because of the form of the vessel. Now you are serving the wine of the Garland Sutra in the vessel of your life, which may or may not be absolutely pure, but in any case is of a form associated with filth. The people will not be able to accept a teaching presented like that.'

The guest changed his way of life.

# MIRRORS

A young and able businessman was hampered in his career by sudden outbursts of fury when he was contradicted in front of others – at a board meeting, for instance. He was making some attempts at spiritual training, and he consulted one of the senior members of the group.

'I know you're going to tell me to count backwards from twenty-nine or something like that, but the fact is that it's so strong that all that just gets blown away. I see a sort of red mist coming in front of my eyes. Isn't there something a bit more positive for people like me?'

The senior looked at him, smartly dressed and clearly very careful about his appearance.

'There might be, for someone like you as you say,' he replied, 'but you have to be willing to get a bit of a shock. Keep a little mirror in your pocket, and when you see that red mist coming up, just go out of the room for a moment and look in the mirror.'

The business man did this next time he was contradicted. When he saw in the glass his face contorted with rage, lips swollen and eyes injected with blood, the ugliness of it was like a shower of icy water.

He never again lost his temper in public.

A teacher was having a meal with two pupils of some years standing, a man and a woman. The man knew that the woman, who had a witty tongue, occasionally used to make amusing but biting comments at the expense of others, and he suspected that she was not above inventing some details to give an extra edge to her little aggressions. Though generally likeable and kind-hearted, she could not resist taking an occasional opening which presented itself.

During the meal, the teacher suddenly launched into a stream of vicious criticisms of someone well-known to all of them, producing wild slanders and accusations which they knew must be untrue. After a little, the two pupils cried out in protest, 'Oh teacher, you *can't* say

# MIRRORS

that!' The teacher's flow stopped as if a tap had been turned off; after a little silence he began calmly to speak of something else.

The two went home thoughtfully. After some weeks, the man noticed that the woman was very careful about her comments in regard to other people; in particular, she never gave rein to her talent for impromptu sarcasms. He realized that she had seen herself in what the teacher had done; he had held up a mirror before her, and because she had done some training, she had been able to realize that it *was* a reflected image, and not a characteristic of the mirror itself. He thought how privileged he had been to be a witness of this spiritually inspired instruction.

A fault, he pondered, of which she had been entirely unconscious, had been brought to light without direct criticism, which might have made her defensive. But how extraordinary that she could have been so completely unaware of it before.

Then he thought, I should not take this as applying to her alone; I should reflect whether I myself have ever at all offended in the same respect. Hardly – I make jokes, of course, but no one could resent . . . well, perhaps once. No – twice. . . . No, more than that . . . oh dear, dear, dear.

And now he thought that perhaps it had been she who had been privileged to be a witness of spiritually inspired instruction.

# FRIED EELS

'You've often told us in your sermons that the Buddha-nature in all is always perfect, and their nature loses nothing even if the mind is disturbed, and gains nothing when the mind is calm. Why then do you tell people to control their passions and acquire peace of mind? On your own showing, nothing real is lost, for the true nature can never be lost or even diminished.'

'They *think* that they lose something, and that causes distress.'

'Then simply tell them nothing has been lost, It is wrong to treat it as if they did lose something by letting their mind run wild, and then tell them how to control it.'

'Let me tell you something that happened to me once. I was passing one of those fried eel shops; you know what a delicious smell there is when they are cooking. I didn't want any eels, but without thinking I inhaled a deep breath and said, "Ah-h-h!" as I passed by.

'A little boy came running after me. "I saw you, I saw you", he cried, 'Daddy says that smell's our business, and I saw you sniffing it up there. You're stealing our business – give it back!"

'"Oh dear, so I am," I told him, "I didn't think. Of course I must give it back" and I let out a big breath slowly, and smiled at him. He went back satisfied; it wouldn't have done to upset him. When he grows up, he'll remember it perhaps and laugh, and maybe think kindly of what he remembers of a Buddhist priest. What harm will that do?'

# A TREMENDOUS LOT

A lecturer on Vedanta made a tour of the towns of northern India, dazzling the audiences with his erudition. He had a phenomenal memory, and his replies to questions were a revelation.

The disciple of a traditional teacher went to one of these lectures, and was much impressed. On his return he asked his teacher about the lecturer: 'Is he really as good as he seems? How much does he really know about Vedanta?'

'Oh, a tremendous lot,' was the answer, 'in fact, everything. And that's all.'

# THE PURE LAND

In China and Japan many millions of Buddhists have been – and in Japan still are – devotees of the Pure Land doctrine. According to this a bodhisattva made a great vow which in time fulfilled itself as the manifestation of the Buddha Amitabha (infinite light), who created a Pure Land paradise in the West for those who would take his name with faith. From this Pure Land it was easy to attain final Nirvana.

An old lady of this faith was walking along the road when she met a Zen master, who said to her,

'On your way to the Pure Land, eh, Granny?'

She nodded.

'Holy Amitabha's there, waiting for you, I expect.'

She shook her head.

'Not there? The Buddha's not in his Pure Land? Where is he then?'

She tapped twice over her heart, and went on her way.

The Zen master opened his eyes wide in appreciation, and said, 'You are a real Pure Lander.'

# THE BRIDGE

A blind man lived in a village in the deep mountains. He was not afraid of the mountain paths, which he had known since childhood, and when spring came and the snows melted, he used to pride himself on the being the first to go to visit his brother in another village not far away, but separated by a deep gorge about twelve feet across. The state maintained a small footbridge across it, consisting of three wide planks driven into the earth on either side, with a small wooden handrail.

One autumn, when the blind man made his last trip that year, he noticed that the planks were becoming shaky, because the earth was crumbling away. He mentioned this to the village headman, who saw the government inspector when he made his rounds. The latter promised that the bridge would be repaired for the next year.

When spring came, however, the blind man had a mild sickness which kept him in bed a week. The village postmaster sent a telegram to the brother so that he should not worry, and when the blind man was up again, he sent another to say that he would definitely pay the visit the next day.

He set out, feeling the warmth of the spring sun, and walking confidently till he came to the bridge. He moved down the little steps cut in the earth, and felt for the bridge with his foot. To his horror he found that there was now only one shaky plank, and no hand-rail at all. He realized that not merely had the old bridge not been repaired, but a winter storm had carried most of it away. However he had sent his telegram, and he was too proud to turn back. He got down on all fours and crawled across, sweating as he heard the cataract roaring below.

When he got to the other side and arrived at his brother's, he told his story.

'But the bridge has been repaired, surely?' said the brother, and they went back the little distance together.

# THE BRIDGE

The brother told him, 'The new bridge is a splendid wide one, driven into solid rock a little further down, just six inches. It's been newly painted. There's a notice up on the bank saying,

> TILL THE PAINT IS DRY,
> PLEASE USE THE PLANK
> WHICH HAS BEEN LEFT FOR YOU.

Of course they knew anyone could easily walk across the plank.'

'Yes,' groaned the blind man, 'Easy if you know that there's a wide bridge six inches below. But if you don't know, it's all you can do to wriggle across clinging to it, and pouring sweat with each inch! It's the same thing: but if you're blind, it's not the same thing.'

# THE FOURTH TRUTH

An enthusiast was explaining about Buddhism to a friend, and told him, 'Perhaps I can best give the spirit of it by one of the traditional stories. The bodhisattva – that is, the Buddha-to-be – was walking past a mountain, pondering the great questions, when he heard a mighty voice crying, "All beings must die." It seemed that heaven and earth were resounding with the words.

'The Buddha-to-be had already realized this truth in his own meditations, and he looked round to see where the voice came from. As his gaze turned to the mountain, the same great voice cried, "This is the law of all existence."

'The Buddha-to-be perceived that the voice came from the top of the mountain; he climbed it, to find that it was an extinct volcano. At the bottom of the crater, deep like an abyss, was coiled a huge dragon. As the Buddha-to-be looked down on it, the dragon opened its great mouth and roared, "There is a way beyond the law of extinction." Then it was silent.

'The Buddha-to-be shouted down, "You have declared three truths, and I have realized these in my own meditations. But I could go no further than this. Is there another truth, is there a fourth truth, which you have not declared?"

'"There is," cried the dragon, "but I am hungry and will not declare it unless I am fed. If you will throw yourself down here to me, I will roar out the fourth truth as you pass through the air, and you will know it for that instant."

'So great was the Buddha-to-be's desire for truth, that he at once threw himself down, and as he fell, the dragon opened his great mouth and roared the last truth, the fourth and final truth. On hearing it, the Buddha-to-be became a Buddha, but his body fell into the dragon's mouth. As it did so, the dragon changed into the form of a god, and caught the Buddha. That was how the Buddha learnt the final truth.'

# THE FOURTH TRUTH

'How wonderful,' said the friend, 'but tell me, what was that fourth and final truth to obtain which the Buddha-to-be was ready to sacrifice his life?'

'Oh. Well, er, I don't remember it just at the moment. But isn't it a beautiful story?'

# THE VASE

A young Brahmachari in India was very high-spirited and tended to be happy-go-lucky in carrying out tasks. The teacher warned him about it, but he found it difficult to change.

One day he said to the teacher: 'Master, in the sermon the other day on karma, you said that if the karma supporting his present life had exhausted itself, a man would die.'

'Yes, that is right.'

'But suppose everyone took very great care of him, surely he could live just a little longer?'

'No; if his span of life has come to an end, it will come to an end.'

'And you said, teacher, that it applies not only to man but to everything.'

'Yes; if a thing's karma is to perish, it must perish.'

'Well,' said the boy, 'I was dusting in the hall this morning, and that vase of Ganges water which you brought back from your pilgrimage, and which you were keeping on the shelf to use to sprinkle on the people at the New Year ceremony – its karma was to be broken and spilt, and it has been broken and spilt. It had to happen, because that was its karma; the karma that supported its existence had come to an end.'

'Yes,' replied the teacher, looking at him, 'It had to happen because the karma that supported it had come to an end. If you had not been so careless dusting that shelf, it would have fallen over anyway; perhaps a monkey would have got into the hall, or there might have been one of those little earthquakes which we have from time to time. It would have happened, certainly. But it happened through *you*, so you are responsible. Your carelessness was the agent through which that karma manifested.

'Now, we are going next week to see those wonderful caves at Ajanta, but as a token of repentance (you are repentant, aren't you?) you had better not go. You can stay at home and meditate on carefulness.'

# THE VASE

The boy's face fell. They had all heard of the wonders of Ajanta.

'However,' continued the master, 'you can think it over, and if by tomorrow afternoon you can give me one sound reason why you should not pay the penalty for your great carelessness, which will result in disappointment for a number of people, then you can go after all.'

The next day the Brahmachari said, 'I cannot find any reason. I was at fault, and I have to accept the penalty, as the result of the bad karma I have created. It is right, I should not go.'

The teacher smiled. 'I will give you a reason. It is true that you have been at fault. And your karma will impose a penalty on you. But there is no reason why I should be the agent through which that karmic result should manifest. You have accepted responsibility, and I can take this opportunity of exercising forgiveness: that will create good karma for both of us. Perhaps the good karma will be, that we shall both see Ajanta.'

# THE SIEVE

A group of devotees invited a master of meditation to the house of one of them to give them instruction. He told them that they must strive to acquire freedom from strong reactions to the events of daily life, an attitude of habitual reverence, and the regular practice of a method of meditation which he explained in detail. The object was to realize the one divine life pervading all things.

'In the end you must come to this realization not only in the meditation period, but in daily life. The whole process is like filling a sieve with water.'

He bowed and left.

The little group saw him off, and then one of them turned to the others, fuming. 'That's as good as telling us that we'll never be able to do it. Filling a sieve with water, I ask you! That's what happens now, isn't it? At least, it does with me. I go to hear a sermon, or I pray, or I read one of the holy books, or I help the neighbours with their children and offer the merit to God, or something like that, and I feel uplifted. My character does improve for a bit – I don't get so impatient, and I don't gossip so much. But it soon drops off, and I'm just like I was before. It *is* like water in a sieve, he's right there. But now he's telling us this is all we shall ever be able to do.'

They pondered on the image of the sieve without getting any solution which satisfied them all. Some thought he was telling them that people like themselves in the world could expect only a temporary upliftment; some thought he was just laughing at them. Some thought he was telling them there was something fundamentally wrong with their ideas. Others thought he might be referring to something in the classics which he had expected them to know; they looked for references to a sieve, without success.

In the end the whole thing dropped away from all of them except one woman, who made up her mind to see the master.

He gave her a sieve and a cup, and they went to the nearby

# THE SIEVE

seashore, where they stood on a rock with the waves breaking round them.

'Show me how you fill the sieve with water,' he said.

She bent down, held the sieve in one hand, and scooped the water into it with the cup. It barely appeared at the bottom of the sieve, and then was gone.

'It's just like that with spiritual practice too,' he said, 'while one stands on the rock of I-ness, and tries to ladle the divine realization into it. That's not the way to fill the sieve with water, or the self with divine life.'

'How do you do it then?' she asked.

He took the sieve from her hand, and threw it far out into the sea, where it floated momentarily and then sank.

'Now it's full of water,' he said, 'and it will remain so. That's the way to fill it with water, and it's the way to do spiritual practice. It's not ladling little cupfuls of divine life into the individuality, but throwing the individuality far out into the sea of divine life.'

# PEARLS BEFORE SWINE

Sometimes from an unexpected quarter one can get a new light on a very familiar phrase, so that it shows a completely different meaning. One of the best-known texts in the Bible is the one about the pearls and swine: 'Neither cast ye your pearls before swine, lest they trample them under their feet, and turn again and rend you.'

Now one can see that the pigs won't value pearls, because they do not know what they are. But why should they turn on you and rend you? I'd always vaguely supposed this was a symbol of mindless malice towards what is felt to be spiritually superior, but that idea must be wrong; if they don't know the pearls are valuable, they won't know there's anything superior to resent.

In 1963–4 I used to take part in a weekly radio dialogue, with a Japanese Buddhist priest, in the studio of the Asahi Broadcasting Corporation in Osaka. He was famous for ruthlessly castigating dishonesty, including the corruption of Japanese politicians of the time. His nickname was 'Poison-tongue', though he was always very pleasant in our interviews. He once said to me, 'If I *don't* say something sharp, people are disappointed.' The Profumo scandal broke when I was there, and he asked why Profumo had had to resign. I said, 'It wasn't because he had a mistress, but because he told a lie to the House of Commons.' To my amazement he shouted, 'Bravo Britain!' I didn't know what to say, and kept quiet. He went on, 'Yes, a British cabinet minister tells one lie and has to resign. But every time a Japanese cabinet minister opens his mouth, it's a lie!' That was the sort of thing he said.

Well, the phrase about pearls and swine came up in one of these discussions. Like many Buddhist priests, he knew the New Testament. The Japanese version is straightforward: 'Do not throw pearls to pigs, for fear they tread them underfoot, and then turn on you and bite you.'

I said, 'It just shows the mindless spite of people who can't understand.'

43

# PEARLS BEFORE SWINE

To my surprise he answered, 'No, it doesn't show that at all. You are condemning the pigs, but Christ is blaming the man who gives teachings too high or difficult for his hearers of that time and place. Pigs aren't vicious. The meaning is: don't throw pearls before swine, because they will think it is food. They try to eat it, but find it is like stones. *Naturally* they are angry and turn on you. It is no fault in the pigs; it is your fault for throwing them what they can't eat. Don't throw pearls to swine: it is not fair on the swine.'

# HELP, NO HELP

Sometimes a new idea can change the whole landscape of endeavour, so to speak; everything appears in quite a different light. This applies in most fields of human activity, but in the case of spiritual endeavours it has some special overtones.

Take the case of doing certain jobs for the spiritual group. Naturally everyone would like to choose their job; someone good at adding would like to do the accounts, and someone good at gardening would like to help in the garden. But, as the Christian saying has it, a cross chosen is not a true cross. To do what one can do well where others can see it is an assertion of personality, and it has not much value as a discipline, though the group may get some benefit from it. (Even that benefit is usually offset by the unconscious arrogance of the expert, perpetually putting others right, or taking things off their hands to do them better.)

Reason-in-the-service-of-the-ego, or Mephistopheles, argues that it must be best to offer one's service in a field where one can make a really significant contribution. But while there is a feeling 'I am making a really significant contribution', training has not begun.

If all goes well, however, some students at least will begin to undertake things which they cannot do well – either at a suggestion from someone, or because they perceive a need. The accountant helps in the garden, perhaps enthusiastically cleaning the stones by scrubbing off moss that has been carefully cultivated for years, and appearing wantonly destructive; the gardener helps with the petty cash and gets the totals wrong, appearing . . . well, after all, where is the money going? Training has begun. Not easy, but then no one ever said it would be.

The service is undertaken in a spirit of offering. For a time it may bring a sort of self-sacrificing joy, but usually it becomes a consciously performed act of dedication to an unpleasant or at least boring task. The performer sees his time out, and then quits with a feeling of 'Well done, thou good and faithful servant.'

But if all goes well, the day comes when the landscape changes. Let me give a concrete example: the cushions, of two sorts, were kept in a large cupboard in one corner of the training hall. There were meetings of different kinds, with different arrangements of the cushions, so shortly before a meeting they were all brought out and arranged in four big piles against one of the walls. Then the arrangers could easily take them and lay them out. To make these preliminary piles was the job of one fairly new member of the sangha. It was also his job to put them away afterwards.

One day when a meeting had just ended, he was told by a senior that there was to be another meeting, of a different and unusual kind, in half an hour. He stood irresolute, and as the senior looked at him he said, 'There's no real point in putting them in piles just for ten minutes, is there? It will be just as easy for them to rearrange them from where they are – probably a lot of them will stay put.'

'Have we something else to do?' asked the other.

'Well, could you tell me something about what came up in the sermon the other day, about the Buddha who lives for a thousand years and the other Buddha who lives for only one day?'

'Yes, certainly,' said the senior, 'and there's a Buddha who only lives for ten minutes', and he began to pick up the cushions and stack them into the usual piles. The two worked together in silence, and in ten minutes the cushions were in their piles perfectly aligned against the wall in the bare hall. They stood back and looked at them, and the senior remarked, 'He only lives ten minutes, but now his life has had its meaning.' Then the other assistants came in and began to take them down to rearrange them.

The moment of looking at the cushions seemed to stand out in the mind of the junior – the cushions brilliantly clear, as if they had been in a shaft of sunlight. After that he did not feel impatient with small chores, or think 'Is it really worth doing?' He felt each time, 'The Buddha lives only so long . . . now his life has been fulfilled.' He felt the Buddha in himself.

And then, gradually, the feeling wore off. He could sometimes revive it by recalling that first moment, but slowly it disappeared as a living inspiration.

This kind of thing very often happens, and people on a spiritual path become familiar with it. Sometimes they get vaguely resentful, and even embittered. When they feel a stir of spiritual life in them, Mephistopheles whispers, 'Remember how many times this has happened before, and remember how it all went off afterwards. Like a little drug, isn't it? You feel better for a bit, but then it goes off and there's a reaction and life is even greyer than before.' There are those who, under the pressure of these insinuations, give up making serious efforts.

It can be a help to look at the same situation in other fields, and for some people a physical example is a good one to awaken a clear awareness of what is going on. My brother was a brilliant amateur golfer, also a fine teacher, who used to be pestered for instruction by a keen 15-handicap golfer with the besetting fault of moving his head several inches during the swing. My brother told me, 'He won't do the training to get a proper balance, because he thinks there's some little secret which will do it all for him. Anyway, I am going to shut him up for a bit.' He apparently directed him to fix a long wooden rod to the side of a shed in his garden, with a metal ring on the end, so that it would lightly press on the top of his head as he took a golf stance. He told him,

'Now practise swinging, but always keeping that ring pressing on your head.'

There was silence from the golfer for several weeks; if they happened to pass he just smiled mysteriously and nodded. I learned that his golf had improved, because his head no longer moved so much.

But some weeks later still, there was a new development. My brother told me, 'He has made another metal ring, just like the one on the stick, and he wears it inside his golf cap. He say it helps to keep his head still.'

I said, 'But that's absurd. The ring will move with his head.'

He said, 'Not completely absurd. As a matter of fact, the feel of it reminds him of when he is in his garden with the stick. It does keep his head relatively still. But it won't last.'

Sure enough, after a month, the golfer was back with his old trouble; perhaps his head was waving about a little less, but it still ruined his golf.

I asked my brother for his analysis, and he told me, 'Well, it was only an idea. At the beginning that idea was associated with the stick, which really did keep his head still. But only in the garden. Then he tried the ring in his cap, and at first the pressure of it was associated only with the garden. So it did keep his head still a lot of the time. But of course, sometimes he moved his head from old habit, and now the pressure of the ring under his cap came to be associated with that as well. Soon it had both associations, and then it wasn't any use to him any more. It was only an artificial means, only an idea. What he has to get is balance, which would keep his head still properly and naturally, but he won't do the practice for that. He'll keep wearing the ring under his cap though. They never give up any of these superstitions. It'll be a good-luck charm, reminding him of the days when he did hit a few straight ones.'

In the same way a spiritual incident, or a text perhaps, can be a great inspiration for a time, but if it remains only an idea, the effect wears off. After that, to keep running it over in the mind is like the golfer's metal ring – only a good-luck charm, without living effect. The ideas are not useless; they can be a great help, and for many an absolute necessity, in waking up in inspiration and energy. But to rely on these fixed things as a substitute for inner life will always lead to disappointment. They are pools, even lakes; whereas what is wanted is a bubbling spring.

J.A

# THE BUDDHA'S FINGERS

A buddhist nun in Japan, who by her strong character, far-sightedness and sympathetic persuasion had a great influence in the community where she lived, was asked how she came to give her life to Buddhism.

She said that she had lost her parents when a small child, and had been brought up by her aunt, a nun in charge of a temple. The aunt was very busy with charitable work, and could not give the child as much time as she would have liked. She took the little girl into the temple and they stood before the Buddha image, seated with the hands joined in the position called Meditation on the Dharma-world. The right hand is laid on the left one, both index-fingers are bent, and the thumb of each hand joins the index finger to form a rough circle.

She presented the child to the Buddha and asked him to watch over her. When they were outside, the aunt said: 'If you feel you have done something wrong, which would make the Buddha angry, at once try to do something good to show your repentance; run and help someone, or do a little bit of cleaning or tidying up. Then go and look at the Buddha. If he is angry with you, his fingers will make two sharp angles.

'If he has forgiven you, they will be the two circles as they are now.'

This made a big impression. 'I can remember many times rushing to the temple and hastily sweeping the garden for a few minutes, and then creeping in, hardly daring to look at the Buddha's fingers. I can't tell you the relief when I saw they were circles, and I knew I was forgiven.'

At this point one of her listeners demurred, arguing:

'I don't approve of using this sort of superstitious falsehood to control the actions of children. They only react against it all when they find out they have been deceived. Didn't you, yourself, have a reaction of anger and scepticism when you found out that the fingers of the Buddha never move at all?'

# THE BUDDHA'S
## FINGERS

The nun replied: 'Oh, it wasn't a falsehood. My aunt would never have told a falsehood. When I found that the Buddha never does move his fingers, I realized that the Buddha always forgives. Even at the moment of weakness or sin, the Buddha forgives. He is never angry. And it made me feel that I didn't want to cause the Buddha to forgive and forgive; I wanted to live so that he would not have to forgive. It was a great help in some crises of temptation and fear. That's what my aunt wanted me to understand by the fingers.'

# GIFTS

In the sermon, the preacher said that a gift must be not only proper in its time and place and recipient, but the heart of the giver must be pure. If there is a desire for recognition, or for a return of any kind, or even just a feeling of superiority, the gift will be tainted, and in the long run will not do the intended good.

Afterwards one of the listeners said to an experienced senior, 'I can't see that. I can understand that something wrong in the heart of a giver might spoil the merit of the gift for *him*, but it won't make any difference to the receiver. If a man's hungry, it doesn't matter to him whether he gets some food from a saint or from the greatest villain alive – he just wants the food.'

The senior made no reply, but began to walk faster on their way home, under the hot sun. The junior felt he would like to stop for a drink at one of the little tea-houses by the side of the road, but the other hurried past. Finally when they were both sweating, the senior paused at a little restaurant and said, 'Wouldn't you like an iced drink?'

They sat down at one of the outside tables, and the proprietor brought the two iced drinks on a tray. The junior could see the beads of water condensed on the outside of the glasses, and his parched throat yearned towards the drink.

'Just a minute,' said the senior, and he went to a little puddle near them, and dabbled his fingers into it. Then he came back, thrust the slimy fingers deep into one of the glasses and passed it across, saying smilingly, 'Lovely and cool!'

# THE BACKHANDER

Traditionally and historically, the Chinese have not been fond of fighting. They have generally rated the warrior's role as something undesirable though sometimes necessary. They could fight well when needed; Confucius remarked, 'I do not like to fight, but if I must fight, I win.' But they do not think that a warrior, for instance, is specially suited for spiritual training, as was thought in India, where the Buddha came from a warrior line, and in Japan, where Zen first came in through the warriors of Kamakura.

In the classic of Tao, one of the most ancient Chinese scriptures, it is said that the fighting man is an ill-omened instrument, and the Way of Heaven has no love for him. Yet sometimes it has to make use of him.

A great Japanese warrior commented on this: 'The bow and arrow, the swords short and long, are unblessed tools of fighting, and of ill omen. Therefore as the Heavenly Way is a way of giving life, and these are the contrary, being means of killing, they really are instruments of ill omen. They can be said to participate in transgression of the Way of Heaven. And yet, when it is unavoidable, making use of them to kill people is also said to be the Way of Heaven. How can this be?

'With the breeze of spring, flowers bloom and their colours vie with each other; with the frost of autumn, leaves fall and the trees are desolate. This is fulfilment and falling away in the Way of Heaven. When a thing is completely fulfilled, Heaven strikes it.

'Man, too, on the tide of fortune, takes to evil; when that evil becomes full, Heaven strikes it. This is when Heaven uses fighting for its ends. Ten thousand people are oppressed by the wickedness of one man, and by killing that one man the other ten thousand are given new life. So there the sword which kills is indeed a blade which gives life.

'There is righteousness in using the arts of fighting in this way.

# THE BACKHANDER

Without righteousness, it is merely a question of killing other people and avoiding being killed by them. Consider carefully what the arts of fighting are for.'

This is like the Western tradition of the 'just war'. Yet, as in the West, there is a tradition of something higher.

The Mongols conquered North China about AD 1230, and in another forty years had control of South China too. Khubilai Khan then prepared two great invasions of Japan, both of which were repulsed by the samurai government of Kamakura. Altogether the fighting in China lasted nearly a century.

Some time towards the end of this period, a great Chinese official sought an interview with a Zen master, and it happened that from the temple they could see the camps of the Mongol conquerors, then preparing yet another campaign.

'The fighting is endless,' lamented the official. 'It goes on and on, and there's no way to stop it.'

'Fighting can be stopped,' said the Zen master.

'How?'

The teacher came up to him and gave him a backhander on the face.

The official was startled and furious . . . This rude old man! . . . the old devil . . . I know I asked him, but what's the point of *that*! . . . I suppose it's one of their damned Zen riddles . . . supposed to have some meaning . . . Idiots! . . . no, it must have some meaning . . . there *must* be some meaning in it . . .

The teacher, who had been looking at him closely, said,

'You stopped it.'

# THE TORTOISE

After the tortoise had won the race against the hare, the other animals began to consult him about improving their running speeds. They had not seen what happened during the race: half of them had been at the start, and the other half at the finishing tape. The first group had seen the hare dashing off into the distance, and the other group had seen the tortoise crawl across the finishing line, and the hare running up second. No one had actually seen the tortoise moving fast, but they came to believe, as the only explanation, that he must have gone into some sort of over-drive during the main part of the race, slowing down when he had passed the hare and was leading by a huge margin. As the animals had no watches, none of them knew just how long the race had taken.

No one listened to the hare's story – a loser always has an excuse.

The tortoise, at first, used to deny that he had any special powers, but they said so often, 'Oh, that's your modesty', that in the end he began to believe in them himself. His friends made him a Victory Medal, which he always wore round his neck. He became more and more confident, and then arrogant, and finally got himself into a situation where he more or less had to challenge the hare to a new match.

'I've done it once, and I'll do it again,' he confided to his friends.

Only the cockatoo, who had flown over the course during the first race and seen what happened, thought the tortoise would lose. The others said to him, 'You're mad; look what he did last time,' and he replied, 'Look what he *is*. He may have won a race, but he's still only a tortoise.'

The day of the race came. When the hare crossed the finishing line, the tortoise had gone six feet three and a half inches. The animals dispersed without looking at each other, as the cockatoo screamed with laughter.

# EIGHTY PER CENT IS PERFECTION

If actions – even the best of actions – are accompanied with the thought 'I am doing good', the benevolent man may become depressed. For instance UN medical teams, working in primitive areas, have greatly reduced infant mortality by giving some simple instructions to the midwives. Yet it was found later that the population of the villages had not increased. The reason was, that there was not enough food to support any more; so the babies saved at birth died a lingering death of starvation a little later.

Even when actions are completely successful in actualizing their hoped-for results, there may be unforeseen and unwelcome effects. A saying of the Soto Zen sect is, 'Eighty per cent is perfection.' They do not explain such phrases, but a parallel comment runs something like this:

'Do things well. But not *very* well. If you do a thing well, others will see it and think, "Yes that is a good job, that is what I should have done if I had been doing it." But if it has been done very well, they may have doubts whether they could have reached that level. Then some of them may try to find something wrong with what you have done. If they cannot find anything wrong with it, they will try to find something wrong with you. If they cannot find something wrong with you, they will invent something. And that is bad for them. So don't put them in that situation.

'There is also the effect on you. If you have done something well, you finish it and forget it. But if you have done it *very* well, you are much more liable to begin to think, "Why, I have done that really very well." And then perhaps your stride will lengthen a little, and your voice will be heard afar. And that will be bad for you.

'So do things well. But if you do them very well, be very careful too!'

# GRACE OF GOD

Some followers of Yoga tend to think that it is somehow 'higher' not to believe in any God.

'There is no God other than the higher self of man,' they say, throwing their heads back proudly. This is fine as long as circumstances go quite well; it sounds all right to a young person, barefoot and more or less permanently camping, who is nevertheless sure of middle-class parents, or at any rate the Welfare State, to fall back on. It may sound all right in a comfortable flat surrounded by imported luxuries. But when in real difficulties, facing serious illness or imprisonment or even heavy responsibilities, it begins to ring hollow. Those who say it may find that they have promoted themselves to the sixth form without being able to tackle the sixth-form syllabus.

The more his spiritual training progresses, the more a student comes to recognize the grace of God. Without some glimpse of it, he is never free from an inner anxiety, however much he may conceal it from others, or even from himself, by bold gestures. While he has the anxiety, he can make little progress. Carefully practised physical relaxation exercises do not remove it, though they may mask its effects for the time being.

Still, mere belief in the grace of God, without spiritual training, can also be a cul-de-sac. This is because the distorted idea of it is used as a cloak for laziness. Like all spiritual ideas, this one has to be thought through right to the end, something which takes considerable courage. An experienced teacher is a great help at these times, because he can bring the hidden obstacles and evasions out into the light.

A man in Japan had an urge to find a spiritual teacher, but after going to see a number of well-known teachers in various towns he had still not found one with whom he could, as it is said, make a 'connection'. One day he happened to hear that a new priest was coming to the neglected temple of Kannon in his own small town.

# GRACE OF GOD

(Kannon is a bodhisattva of compassion, who perceives the appeals for help of all beings in their distress, and whose wisdom find ways to help them, sometimes miraculously. The name Kannon means the one who perceives the voices.)

When this seeker entered the temple and met the new priest, he had an experience like an electric shock, and realized that this was to be the temple where he could focus the devotion which he now felt for the first time.

He attended the services regularly, and spent some of his spare time and money helping to clean and repair the temple. After some weeks of this, the priest said to him,

'You should now begin to repeat the invocation of holy Kannon for an hour every day: I can show you how to do it. Every Buddhist must do some form of meditation, and this can be the form for you.'

These words jarred on the new devotee. He made no reply, but a few days later when they were tidying up after the morning service, he said to the priest,

'It seems to me that to undertake practices like invocation would be to deny the grace of holy Kannon, which brought me here. All my searches were of no avail; it was when I was not searching, not making any personal human efforts, that by the grace of Kannon you came here, by the grace of Kannon I heard about it, and by the grace of Kannon I had that experience which has changed my life. Am I now to say to holy Kannon "I shall resume my personal efforts again, as your grace may not suffice to take me the rest of the way"?'

The priest made no reply, but invited him to stay on for the midday meal. This was generally a simple affair of rice and a couple of vegetables; that day, however, after hearing his invitation accepted, the priest gave some money to his wife with a few whispered words, and when the lunch was served it included some rare dainties, deliciously cooked. The man felt his mouth water as it was set before him. The priest said the usual invocation to Kannon, and then he and his wife immediately began to eat without waiting for their guest. When the latter looked at the tray before him, he found to his surprise that there were no chopsticks on it. For a while he was too embarrassed to say anything, but as they did not seem to notice that he was not eating, he finally blurted out,

'Excuse me, but . . . there are no chopsticks.'

'Chopsticks?' said the priest wonderingly, 'Whatever would you want with chopsticks?'

'Why, I need them to pick up the food.'

'Surely you are not intending to pick up that food, are you?' said the priest with an expression of surprise. 'That would be a denial of the kindness of my wife, who has got this special food for you, and cooked it specially for you, and set it out on the tray for you, and brought the tray for you, and put it in front of you. If you now say you want chopsticks, you are as good as saying that her service is not complete. Surely you should wait till she puts it in your mouth, shouldn't you?'

The man turned scarlet, and hung his head. The wife gently put a pair of chopsticks on the tray, and the priest patted his arm and said, 'Please eat your meal and enjoy it.'

That night the guest asked for instructions in how to say the invocation of Kannon, which the priest gave him with great affection, adding, 'What you cannot do by your own power, holy Kannon will always do for you; but this little thing which you can do, the holy Bodhisattva leaves for you out of courtesy, so that you can have the joy of cooperating with the One who sees the cries of the whole world, and helps the distress of those who utter them.'

# WILL OF GOD

Allied to the doctrine of the grace of God is the doctrine of the will of God, and this too can be a stumbling block to those who use it as an excuse. A famous judge in India, at the end of the last century, was well-known as a devotee of God, and once a thief who was brought before him tried to make use of the fact. The charge was completely proved and the thief made no attempt to deny it, but said instead, 'Your Honour, I only wish to say this. When the opportunity came to steal that, I felt an irresistible impulse to do it, and I thought to myself that it must be the will of God that I should steal it. And it *was* the will of God, surely, Your Honour, because otherwise it couldn't have happened.'

'Are you denying that you had any responsibility?' asked the judge.

'All I'm saying, Your Honour, is that it must have been the will of God or it couldn't have happened. When I felt that impulse coming up in me, surely I was right to bow my head before the will of God?'

'God gives us many impulses,' said the judge, 'And he gives us the power of choosing between them, so that we may show our reverence for his commandments, and our love of our fellow-men.'

'But he gave me *this* impulse,' riposted the thief. 'I have heard that Your Honour says God is in each man, playing different roles. Well, one of the names of holy Shiva is thief . . .'

'He is called thief because he steals our sins, but you were stealing things belonging to poor people.'

'It is stealing just the same. In that little shop, in the middle of the night, I was the Lord as Shiva, and my role was the thief.'

'Reverence to the Lord, in the little shop, in the middle of the night, acting out the role of thief,' said the judge slowly. 'But here in my little court, in the day, the Lord is playing a different role. Yours is a petty crime, but I have a wide discretion. I feel rising in me an impulse to impose on you the heaviest sentence' – his voice began to boom – 'because in me He is playing the role of the just ruler, the mighty controller and orderer of the universe. Reverence to the Lord in the form of the great terror, the upraised thunderbolt, which preserves order in the world!'

'Stop, stop!' cried the thief, 'I withdraw my plea. Please treat me as a sinful human being.'

The judge laughed and gave him a light sentence.

J.A

# TEA

Not long ago, a Japanese Tea Ceremony master made a visit to a certain foreign country to give demonstrations. His hosts found a beautiful garden, with two pavilions in it. In one the guests were to assemble, and then a group of fifty would go to the other pavilion, where the master was to demonstrate the ceremony. After about forty minutes, the audience would change; those who had witnessed it went back, and a new group walked the hundred yards to the master's pavilion to see a new performance.

He commented when he returned to Japan, 'In that country the men shout and the women scream. When I heard the very first group coming across, shouting and screaming, I thought, "These people will never understand the spirit of Tea." But to my amazement, they sat very still and attentive, and there was a good atmosphere. I thought, "They have understood the spirit of Tea after all." They left quietly, but as they re-crossed to the first pavilion, they burst out, shouting and screaming just as before. I felt quite discouraged, and that my time had been wasted.

'But then I thought, "No, that is wrong. They will never be the same again. They have been able to sit still, in peace, for half-an-hour. Now their old habits have taken hold again, but they will remember, in a corner of their mind, that half an hour of peace. And one day, perhaps years afterwards, when they feel deeply disturbed over something, they will think back to that time of Tea, and it will help them." '

# CHAINS

A man said to his teacher, 'I have tried to break my habit of going to wine-shops and brothels, but I can't do it. I am in chains to my nature. You can't expect a man in chains to do anything.'

The teacher met him going to the town one evening. He was smartly dressed and walking briskly in anticipation.

The teacher said, 'You don't look like a man in chains.'

# THE BLUE CLOTH

Sometimes in a spiritual group a dispute develops over practically nothing. Although it is so trivial, people feel strongly about it. No one seems to know the cause of what is happening, or what to do.

When the teacher first founded the group they were poor, and had only a cheap brown cloth over the altar on which was the form of the god. They worshipped with prayers and mantras for the first half of the meeting, and then, when the minds were to some extent pacified, they meditated on the Upanishadic text: 'O holy divinity, I am what thou art, and thou, O holy divinity, art what I am.'

The teacher had once mentioned that to see or meditate on the colour blue has a calming effect on the mind, and added that blue was the best colour for an altar cloth. This remark was taken down, but nothing was done at the time because they were so poor. Then it was forgotten.

Many years later, a new member reading over the old records came across it. He bought a blue silk cloth, and had it beautifully embroidered with the mantra of the divinity. He presented it to the man whose responsibility was the altar cloth, who accepted it without comment and put it away. But an old brown cloth continued to be used.

The new member tried to accept this, but after a few weeks he went to the head disciple, told him what had happened, and said,

'I can't worship, I can't concentrate on the prayers, I can't keep my mind on the mantra, I can't meditate. All the time I'm thinking of that altar cloth and saying to myself, it's wrong, it's wrong, it's wrong.'

So the chief disciple went to the altar-cloth man and said,

'Now you have to accept this. He can't focus his mind because this little thing has become a great thing to him.'

'But this is against our whole tradition. We've always had a brown cloth. The teacher may perhaps have said something about a blue

# THE BLUE CLOTH

cloth, just in passing, but very likely it was taken down incorrectly. We've *always* had a brown cloth. If we give way on this point, there will be pressure to change another one too, and in the end nothing of the tradition will remain.'

'Now we've both been here a long time, haven't we? And we know what our teacher thinks of rituals – just a little to help calm the mind, but no reliance on them. And this which is happening is disturbing his mind; he hasn't enough experience to learn from it. Please accept this business as it has happened, and put the blue cloth on the altar each time.'

Now the splendid embroidered blue cloth was on the altar each time the group met. It was much admired. After a few more weeks, the new member again asked for an interview with the head disciple, who said, 'What is it now? You have what you want.'

'Yes,' was the bewildered reply. 'But I still can't worship, I can't concentrate on the prayers, I can't keep my mind on the mantra, I can't meditate. All the time I'm seeing that altar cloth and thinking to myself, it's right, it's right, it's right.'

'Ah,' said the chief disciple. 'It's good that you're aware of what's happening. Well now. We'll put the old cloth back until it's worn out, and then in the natural way we'll replace it, with the blue one. Perhaps we've both learnt from this. We have learnt about the blue cloth – that's something valuable that had got overlooked somehow. And you, perhaps you've learnt something too? It's easy to fall into worshipping an altar cloth.'

# SWEEPING

A foreigner applied to enter a Zen temple. He had made no preparations, and could neither sit in the formal posture without pain, nor understand what was said. The teacher told him, through the interpreter, that it would be a very hard time. He persisted and finally was allowed to come in.

As usual in such cases, he felt that he must make a special contribution to the life of the temple, and all he could do was the physical work. He made it a rule to get up very early and undertake the daily chores, beginning with sweeping the garden.

He discovered that the head monk did not always rouse the monks at the fixed time; sometimes he let them sleep on, when they had had a difficult day. The foreigner, however, was always up. Slowly he came to resent the fact that others were not following the rule as he was. He wrote a short account of the experience afterwards, in which he said that he was beginning frankly to hate the monks as he worked and they slept. When he came to near the sleeping quarters, sometimes his broom would accidentally knock the verandah.

When his anger reached boiling point he spoke to the teacher, who said, 'Why are you doing this?'

He said, 'I am following the rule as part of my spiritual training.'

'If it is simply a question of your own spiritual training, it does not matter to you what the others do or do not do. There must be something else.'

'Well, I suppose in a way I am setting an example – an example which I am afraid is entirely wasted.'

'The example you are setting is sweeping and cleaning in a spirit of pride and resentment. That is not a good example, and it is right that it is not followed.'

'How should one set an example, then?'

'When the Buddha gets up, and picks up the Buddha broom, and sweeps the Buddha dust from the face of the Buddha earth, and no one knows about it – there is the example which will have an effect.'

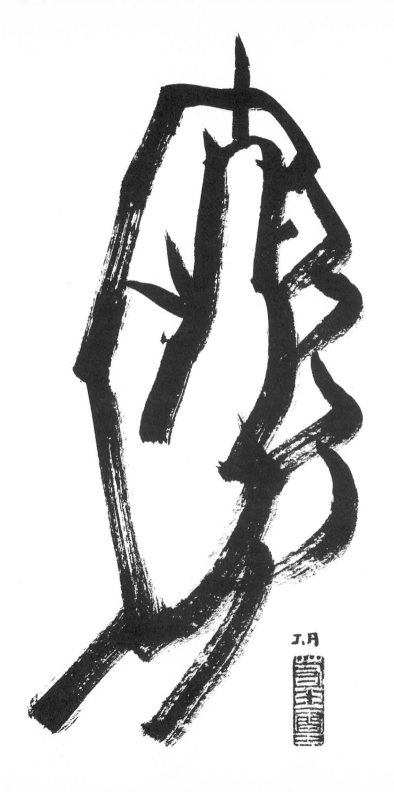

# THE NEEDLE IN THE HAYSTACK

A spiritual teacher in India said to two pupils: 'Imagine that what you are seeking is represented by an iron needle buried somewhere in a haystack. You must find that needle. Think it over, and tell me tomorrow how you would go about looking for it – this will give you an insight into the spiritual search.'

When they came back the next day, one said: 'I should set fire to the haystack and watch it burn to ashes, and then wait for the wind to blow them away. In the end I should see the needle lying before me.'

'That is the path of the recluse,' commented the teacher, 'who gives up everything. It is a true path if heroically pursued right to the end – but from one point of view it might seem a pity to waste all the hay.'

Then the other pupil gave his answer: 'I should take the straws one by one from the stack, look at each and feel it with my fingers, and put it behind me. Finally I must find the needle, even if I have to transfer the whole haystack from in front of me to behind me.'

'That is the path of pure philosophical analysis,' said the teacher. 'It too is a true path; each incident, each thought, of the haystack of life, is scrutinized carefully as it passes from future to past time; it is seen clearly and then put aside. The path requires immense patience and detachment, combined with a power of continuous awareness.'

'Is there any other way?' they asked.

'There is. It makes use of yet another fact about the iron needle. One of you took advantage of the power of iron to survive fire; relative to the hay, it is immortal. The other one used the fact that iron has a certain colour, and that it is hard in the fingers. But there is something else about the thing you are looking for, which is, that it is magnetic. And this is something which the seeker can acquire also. If you spend some time creating a powerful magnet, then suspend it on a thread from your hand and walk round the haystack, pausing frequently to stand quite still, after not very long there will be a tiny quiver in the magnet you hold. (There is a quiver too in the iron you are seeking, but you do not know about that.) If you follow the tiny movement of your magnet, it will become stronger. If you do not follow it, it will disappear. Following the path so indicated, you will be drawn directly to where the needle is hidden; with a little digging you will come close to it. Then the magnet you hold and the needle you are seeking will leap joyously to become one, and your search will be rewarded.

'In our ancient Sanskrit language, one word for magnet is ayas-kanta-mani, which means the mani or precious stone which is loved by iron, and which loves iron. Create and cultivate a great love in yourself for what you are spiritually seeking, using the traditional forms which are given to you for just that purpose. Know that the quiver of love in you is being met by a quiver of love from the Beyond. If there were no quiver of love there, you would feel no quiver of love here, just as the magnet would not tremble unless there were also a response in the iron. The attraction of love, as you develop it in yourself, will lead you, and become stronger and stronger. At first you will perceive it most clearly when you are very still in meditation, like the man standing very still holding the magnet; but soon you will feel it all the time. You will still have to do some digging into your haystack, but you will know where to dig. Finally what you are longing for will leap joyously to meet you, and you will leap joyously to meet it, and you will become what you have been seeking.'

# INCREDIBLE

Many people searching for some reality above the ordinary experience of the world tend to think of things of the spirit as a sort of package deal. One may practise Buddhist meditation as a means of attaining spiritual insight and independence, but then one is in duty bound, as it were, also to believe in palmistry (Western and Eastern, though the principles are entirely different), astrology, geomancy, and so on. Apart from the fact that the Buddha himself forbade such practices, there are many disadvantages in the attitude of 'It's all true, and more.'

The Chinese saying is, that wherever the people gather, there the pickpockets too will come, and this is true of spiritual things. Oddities of thought are built up into fantastic systems, skilfully peddled to credulous people who end up bitterly disappointed. A man in one of the great cities of the East, who had a reputation as a sort of magician, used to begin an interview by asking the client to bare the right forearm and lay it on the table. Then he used to place on it a little tripod made of cardboard with a sort of horizontal windmill on top, which could freely revolve. He told the client to sit quite still. There was no possible source of power within the little machine, every detail of which was clearly visible, but quite soon the top would begin to revolve. The magician used to scrutinize the movement for a minute or so, and then proceed with the interview. He never explained it, but the clients were duly impressed. One of them, a European woman with a deep interest in Buddhism, once described it to a friend who was an engineer. From her account, he constructed a similar toy, and showed her that the currents of warm air, rising from the body-heat of the arm, would be sufficient to make the little windmill rotate. She was terribly upset at having been tricked, as she felt, and gave up not only her visits to the magician, but her interest in Buddhism as well. She had thought of it all as a package deal; she had believed everything, and now found she could believe nothing.

There is a folk tale which illustrates the point amusingly but profoundly. It comes from Jammu in northern India. In the troubled times which followed the collapse of the Mogul Empire, rich people buried jewels in the ground, hoping to come back later to retrieve them. Sometimes they were never able to do so and the secret died with them. In a Jammu village, a husband and wife, digging in their garden one afternoon, unearthed a large ruby. To declare their find would have meant that the village bully would simply have come and taken it from them; their only chance was to wait till the husband made his usual monthly trip into the city, where he had a relative who was a jeweller. Then he might hope for a fair price for it. But unfortunately their little five-year-old son had seen the ruby dug out, and they knew he would be bound to tell everyone. What could they do? They could not tie his tongue, or keep him indoors for the next month.

It is not easy to think of a solution, and in a spiritual tradition the teacher will sometimes break off this kind of story, telling the pupils to think out something for the parents to do. When they have wrestled with it for quite a time, they are able to appreciate the conclusion of the story, and apply it to their own lives. Readers who are interested might try laying this book aside, and pondering what they would have done in place of the parents.

What the mother did was, to keep the little boy in the house that evening. After he had gone to bed she went next door and borrowed the oven to make some cakes with some very special honey which she had been keeping for a long time for a future treat. Just before dawn she got up quietly and scattered some of these cakes on the roof, and others in the garden. Then she woke her son and said, 'This is a lucky day – it's been raining cakes on our house. Get up quickly and help me

# INCREDIBLE

pick them up before the birds get them.' By the light of the pale dawn moon, the two of them gathered up the cakes into bags; they had some of them at breakfast. Then she let her son go out.

Sure enough, when he was with some of his friends in another part of the village, he blurted out, 'We dug up a big shiny red stone in the garden yesterday.' The bully's wife happened to be there, and she pricked up her ears and listened carefully. 'Yes,' he went on, 'and that's nothing. It rained cakes on us too in the night; I got up with mummy this morning and helped her pick them up. I bet you've never had cakes rain on your house.' As the children discussed this, some believing and others doubting, the listener relaxed, laughing. The merely rare event was now associated for her with the impossible, and she dismissed the whole thing. She could not believe in the cakes, quite rightly, and because they were associated in her mind with the ruby, she did not believe in that either.

# QUALIFICATION

The king of a small state in the south of India used to meditate every day on himself as a servant of God. He limited the satisfaction of his desires to what he thought appropriate to a servant, and practised a servant's simplicity of life. After some years, this practice produced in him extraordinary energy and clear-sightedness; his kingdom was a success internally, and the neighbouring kings soon found it did not pay to venture to extend their territory.

The king's spiritual adviser (though not his teacher) was one of his ministers to whom the king owed, and knew that he owed, a good deal of his success. This minister was an advanced practicant of meditation.

One day the king learned, by chance, that the minister's own form of meditation was on the self as infinite shining space. He told the minister that he would like to go on to this higher form of meditation, but the minister advised him against it.

'It would not accord with your present role,' he told him.

The king was a little put out, and retorted, 'If you can say this and meditate on it, I can do so too. Why shouldn't I?'

The minister said, 'You can say it, of course. But it will not have any effect unless the one who says it is qualified for it.'

'What has qualification to do with it?' cried the king. 'The words are bound to have their effect.'

The minister beckoned to the king's bodyguard, who stood on the far side of the room. The man came running up and stood at attention.

'Slap his face!' said the minister in a firm voice.

The bodyguard's jaw dropped in astonishment.

'You heard me, didn't you? Slap his face!' ordered the minister sharply.

The bodyguard closed his mouth firmly and stood motionless, his eyes fixed on the king.

# QUALIFICATION

The minister turned to the king: 'You say it.'

'Slap his face,' said the king in a low voice. Instantly the bodyguard's hand landed in a loud smack on the minister's cheek. The king waved him away – 'Not so hard, not so hard.'

After a little silence, the minister said quietly, 'You see? We spoke the same words, but you were qualified, and I was not. So the words you spoke were effective. But what I said would not have been effective, even if I had repeated them a thousand times, because I did not have the qualification to say them. It's the same with spiritual truths.'

# DRUNK

A great spiritual teacher used to live in obscurity as a beggar, and his pupils did the same. One disciple, a good speaker, having completed the training and received his teacher's mandate, began speaking in market-places. His words had a tremendous effect, and the ecclesiastical authorities made inquiries about him. In the end they found out what a great teacher he had had, and pressed him to accept a high office.

The teacher in his poor clothes came to the inauguration ceremony, and, looking at the magnificence in which his disciple was now robed, said, 'You don't need those things to tell people the holy Truth. It's a sort of intoxication – you and them both.'

Thereafter the disciple, even when he became what corresponds to an archbishop, dressed as plainly as he could. But for a big ceremony he had to wear one of the splendid formal robes. On one occasion he was passing, magnificently dressed, in a procession on the way to a great temple where there was to be an important ordination rite. A beggar stood watching them go by. The attendants were amazed when suddenly the door of the litter was thrown open and the gorgeous embroideries dragged in the dust as their wearer prostrated himself at the feet of the beggar.

The beggar picked him up, looked at him with affection and muttered, 'Drunk again!'

# MEDITATION

A man used to complain to his teacher that he couldn't meditate. 'I can't hold my thought on it for long – I start thinking what we will be having for breakfast, or some argument we've had in the family, or whether I shall be transferred at work.'

One day the teacher suddenly blazed up and shouted, 'I'm the fool, to have taken on a fool like you at all! I'm going to finish with you – why should I go on? Come back tomorrow, and unless you can give me one good reason why I should still see you, you can take your things and go.'

The pupil tried to stammer an apology, but the teacher cut him short and physically pushed him out.

That night he could not sleep: he was wondering what he could do to get the teacher to keep him on. Next day he brought a present for him, and timidly gave it to the attendant, who then announced his name.

The teacher came out quickly and said, 'Come in and sit down. How have you been?.

He answered, 'I could not sleep for thinking how I could appeal to you – *please* keep me on. I can't give any reason, but please keep me as your pupil.'

'You couldn't sleep for thinking about it? That's good. That's what you needed,' the teacher told him. 'When you have trouble with your mind, think back to that, and meditate with the same earnestness. You've learnt what it means to meditate.'

# THE WAY OF THE MERCHANT

Be your concern with action alone, never with results.
  Let not the fruit of action be your motive, nor yet be
  attached to inaction.

Steady in yoga do your actions, casting off attachment;
  Be the same in success and failure. Evenness of mind is
  yoga. (*Gita* II. 47. 48)

In some countries of the East, the merchant was not highly regarded. He was thought to be dominated by selfish profit, and lacking in the inner strength of the warriors and the calm of the priestly class.

A young warrior got to know a merchant in his city; something about this man's character attracted him. Once he went to sympathize after the merchant had suffered a big loss, but he found him not at all disturbed, and another time when he knew that a minister had made important purchases from the merchant, the latter did not mention the matter at all.

One day when they were walking together, they saw a fire and helped to rescue the family, the merchant showing a calm daring which impressed the warrior. He said afterwards:

'You will excuse my saying this, but it was rather unexpected to see you calmly taking such risks; I had thought that came from the way of the warriors alone.'

'Oh,' replied his friend, 'merchants have a way of their own.'

'I suppose you pray to Ganesha to protect you? All you merchants worship the Lord of Prosperity.'

'I do worship Ganesha, but I never ask for anything. To pray for things is all right for little merchants who are not yet on our way; however much he may own, if he prays for things, he is only a little merchant. If I prayed for something, I should always be anxiously

# THE WAY OF
# THE MERCHANT

wondering whether my prayer would be answered or not. That would disturb my heart, and no one with a disturbed heart can be a great merchant.'

'Please tell me about your way,' asked the warrior.

The merchant looked serious and said, 'Words are no use in explaining the way. But I can show you. A little further on there is a shop where the owner is ignorant but cunning. When a great man dies suddenly, he immediately goes to the house and makes an attractive offer for small things in the dead man's effects; often the relatives think them of no value, and in the confusion he may get a good bargain. But as he himself does not know the value of the things either, he waits till a prospective buyer comes in, and then takes his cue from how much interest the customer shows.

'When he sees me coming, he will be on the alert, because he knows I am well informed in such things. He has a little box which is really valuable because it is one of a set with a long history, which has got dispersed; he bought it cheap from an old widow who knew nothing about it. I have the others, and this one would complete the set.

'Of course I could send an agent to buy it, but a great merchant never does anything like that. He goes himself, without any tricks.'

When they got to the shop, the merchant looked around a little, and then inquired, 'How much for this box?' The proprietor looked narrowly at him, and named a high price.

'What!' smiled the merchant. 'For that little box?'

'It might be one of a set . . . perhaps?'

'I am not buying a set. I should not pay more than a quarter of what you're asking; even that would probably be much more than you paid for it. Well, I have no concern with it – keep it,' and he walked away down the street with his friend.

As they rounded the corner, talking cheerfully of other things, the

# THE WAY OF
# THE MERCHANT

shop-owner came running after them. 'I have always had a respect for you, and I have decided to let you have it at a quarter of my price, as you wanted. But I hope you will remember this gesture of friendship.' The merchant paid without comment, and took the box.

Afterwards the warrior said, 'But you told me a great merchant never used tricks. That was a trick, nothing more than a trick.'

'Do you think so? Let us see whether it was or not. Is there anything in any shop which you have had your eye on?'

'Yes – there is an old sword in a shop near here; it must have belonged to one of the noble Rajput families, because the hilt is very small. We pride ourselves on our small hands; our enemies may take the weapons from our dead bodies, but they cannot use them. I should like that sword, but I doubt whether I could afford it.'

'Well, you can try the trick then. I will leave you; come in and and see me afterwards.'

When they met again, the warrior was looking down.

'It didn't work,' he said. 'I did exactly what you did; I told him I wouldn't pay more than a quarter what he asked, and that I had no concern with it. I am sure he does not know the real value of it, but he didn't come after me. I kept hoping he would, but he didn't. It would have been wonderful to have that sword in my family; it's one of the old ones.'

'Then you are still concerned with it, aren't you? I told you words are no good in the way. Now sit here, and give up that sword. Give it up completely.'

They sat in silence for a time, and then the warrior said quietly, 'I can't. Tell me how to do it.'

The merchant replied. 'For the sake of honour you would be willing to give up your life in the way of the warrior. But this is the way of the merchant. Every day I sit before the image of Ganesha, and

# THE WAY OF THE MERCHANT

I meditate that all around me, my shop and my goods and my house and my warehouses, everything I have has caught fire and is burning away. Even my body catches fire. The whole world catches fire, and burns and burns till everything is ashes.

'Then there is only Ganesha and I, I and Ganesha, Ganesha and I, in the whole world. Perhaps there is something still further, but it can't be spoken.'

One day a friend said to the young warrior, 'Why do you go around with that merchant? You are a warrior, and he is a merchant; honest, I admit, but still just a merchant after all.'

'He certainly acts like one,' was the reply, 'but I don't know that he is just a merchant. It seems to me sometimes that it is not really a merchant there at all, but Ganesha playing at being a merchant.'

# POWERS

In the great Yoga classic of Patanjali it is stated that a man who practises virtue and does not hate those who do not (sutra I.33) can acquire various powers (sutra III.23) such as a knowledge of remote or concealed things (sutra III.25), by making special concentrations on them. But in sutra III.37 it goes on to say that such 'perfections' are obstacles to spiritual progress and lead to relapses, because the excitement they cause will disturb and darken the mind which exercises them.

Many people find it rather irritating to hear these things being mentioned and then immediately ruled out on grounds which are not necessarily convincing. They usually think they would do rather well if they could exercise real power, such as that of a leader of some great movement.

The head of a large Buddhist sect was once asked by a reporter whether it is difficult for a man in a position of power to remain humble and kind.

'Usually very difficult,' was the reply.

'But you yourself have this position at the head of more than ten thousand temples – do you find . . .?'

'I have to remind myself occasionally, of course, but the fact is that in a public position like this every little thing I do is seized on by the press and ruthlessly criticized. So there is not too much danger that I shall begin to think myself in any way remarkable. As for kindness, well there again I have to meet the approval of the followers of this sect, and set an example to them. So I am not likely to be allowed to become tyrannical in my present position.'

'Then why do you say it is difficult?'

'Ah, that is something else. That is when there is *real* power. I had it once, when I had completed my second year in the training temple. I was asked to train a new entrant from the country in how to cook. I was a good cook myself – mother had often been ill and I had had to

# POWERS

learn it. Well, that boy was clumsy and had no idea how to go about things. I gave him absolute hell. There were just the two of us in the kitchen most of the time; there was no one to know about it, and he was too scared to complain. Gradually he got paler and paler, and finally the head monk realized something must be wrong. He transfered him to the garden, where he soon recovered. Now that was a situation of real power. And I didn't do very well in it. I simply didn't understand what I was doing. I used to tell myself that strict training was necessary. I realized soon afterwards that I had been arrogant and cruel, and it has been a lesson to me all my life.'

There may be other disadvantages attached to acquiring unusual powers. A merchant, who had done a good deal of unselfish charity in strict secrecy, one day met a yogi who looked at him and said,

'You have laid up a store of good karma. You are entitled to receive some instructions, by which you can either make spiritual progress or get one of the occult powers.'

'I am not sure I am ready for spiritual progress,' said the merchant, 'in fact, I don't know what it is. But I could do with the ability to know the thoughts of others; I wouldn't use it to swindle them, but only to protect myself from being cheated.'

The yogi said, 'This is easily learned, but perhaps you had better have a little experience of it first. When I came to this village, I passed a little hut in disrepair at the northern end; please go and stay for three days and nights there.'

The merchant took an umbrella to protect himself against leaks, and a stove to cook his meals; he more or less camped in the little hut for three days and nights. When he returned he looked tired and harassed.

'What happened?' said the yogi.

'Why, it was a failure. I didn't become able to read thoughts. The fact is that I haven't been able to sleep. In the house just by my hut there's a pair who are both drunkards and very quarrelsome. They were swearing and shouting and screaming at each other all day and night; I couldn't sleep, and even in the day I couldn't read, it was so disturbing. I don't understand why you sent me there.'

'Yes, I heard all this in passing when I first came here,' said the yogi. 'But you did know their thoughts, didn't you? They were shouting them. I wanted you to have that experience – that's what it would be like. Voices yelling in your head all the time.'

'Surely one could learn to switch off the telepathy by mental control, couldn't one?' asked the merchant. 'Then it would do one no harm.'

'That is true. So you could begin now practising how to withdraw your attention from external disturbances; it will help you to make real spiritual progress. But when you can spend three days and nights in that hut without being disturbed, switching off your attention by mental control, then if you like I will teach you telepathy. It may take you quite a few years.'

The merchant thought for a bit, and then laughed.

'Tell me about real spiritual progress,' he asked, 'not this stuff.'

# THE DOOR

One wing of the palace abutted on a rubbish heap; there was the outline of a door faintly to be seen on the wall. It was rumoured that each year the king stood for an hour behind the door, and if anyone asked for admittance, he took him in. It was not said what the king would do then.

A merchant was wronged by a minister, but could not prove his case. He abandoned the rest of his property, and stood day and night in front of the outline of the door, every hour asking for admission in the hope that sometime the king would be there.

At first he nearly died of hardship. Then a passing horseman threw him an old straw coat, and a beggar brought him some scraps. The city people heard of him, and came to see the man standing in front of the wall. Some laughed, but others were impressed at the way he had sacrificed everything to get justice. A few stalls went up to serve refreshments to strangers who came to see the sight. Admirers built him a hut, and then a larger building. Others came to serve him. He was regarded as the embodiment of justice, and people brought their disputes to be settled, instead of going to the courts. His decisions were universally admitted to be fair and wise.

One midnight it seemed there was a crack of light in the wall, and a faint voice said, 'Enter!' He looked back and saw the sleeping people who would seek his help next day. He quietly finished his salutation and returned to his usual place.

# THE CALLIGRAPHER

Tesshu was one of the most famous calligraphers in Japan at the end of the nineteenth century. Unlike other masters, he would write for anyone, and never looked at the fee which they might offer. He threw all the envelopes, unopened, into a chest in his hall; when someone came in need, he opened them one after another until he had the required amount to meet the asked-for loan or gift.

A butcher once boldly asked him whether he would write a sign-board for his shop. The master's disciples were horrified – a tradesman asking for a masterpiece to hang in the street to increase his business!

Tesshu said, 'Will it improve the appearance of the street?'

'Of course,' they said, 'But he is not thinking of that, but purely of money, purely of money.'

The master said, 'Probably he does feel that a sign written by me will make money, and *you* are certainly thinking about money. But I am not thinking about money.'

He wrote it, and a Tokyo street became beautiful.

Tesshu once, in an emergency, borrowed a thousand yen from a moneylender. This was given on the word of a former samurai, but when the moneylender thought it over, he decided to ask for a formal acknowledgment of the debt. The master at once agreed and wrote on a large sheet of paper, in his wonderful calligraphy:

> The classics say that each man has seven bad habits, and one of mine is a reluctance to repay a debt. In view of this bad habit, by giving this acknowledgement for this loan, I now rule it out and make the repayment of the money a little more possible.

He passed it over, and when the moneylender saw it he lost colour, seeing which the master clapped his hands and gave a great laugh. The moneylender had to take it and went slowly home.

# THE CALLIGRAPHER

One of his acquaintances, however, happened to notice the paper. He looked at it carefully and then said, 'This is something quite out of the ordinary, both in its phrasing and the calligraphy; I will take it off you for a thousand yen, if you like.' The moneylender suddenly realized what he had, and had it framed.

When the time came for Tesshu to return the money and he told the other to collect it, the moneylender said,

'I make a gift of it in exchange for the master's writing,' and would not take it. He kept Tesshu's receipt as an heirloom.

# OBSTACLES

A man asked the abbot of a monastery outside a city whether he could come each weekend to meditate there, as at home in the city there were constant hindrances and the noise from the street interrupted his meditation. 'You may come,' said the abbot, 'but there will still be interruptions.' The man came the next weekend, and in the afternoon entered the great meditation hall, all alone. The place was absolutely silent, and quite bare except for a small image of the Bodhisattva of Wisdom at one end, with a single stick of incense burning in front of it. In the dim peace he felt his nerves relax and sat down to try to enter his meditation. After a little the place felt almost *too* silent; he thought he heard a tiny sound and opened his eyes a little. He noticed the stick of incense, and began to wonder why the smoke always rises. Then he noticed the perfume of the incense, far superior to the incense in the temple near his home. He speculated how much it might cost, and thought: 'If it is not too expensive (and probably they get quite a reduction for buying in quantity) perhaps I could buy some from them here at cost price – they are after all spiritual men and not interested in profit – and then sell it to the priest at our temple and make a little for myself,' The bell sounded, and he realized that his meditation hour was finished. He went straight to the abbot, prostrated himself and said: 'I understand. The interruptions are from within. From now on I shall practise meditation in my home. Please give me your blessing.' The abbot blessed him, and he returned.

# KARMA

The teacher in his sermon was explaining the doctrine of karma, which teaches that all voluntary actions produce an effect on the doer in this or future lives. 'If you want to know what you have done in the past,' he said, 'look at your present circumstances, which are the result of what you did; if you want to know what your future will be, look at what you are doing now, which will shape it. In the Christian Bible too the same doctrine is hinted at in the words, "As you sow, so shall you reap." '

Afterwards one of the pupils said to the teacher, 'In the Christian Bible there is a story of the man who was attacked and left for dead by robbers. Two people passed by on the other side of the road, and then a third man picked him up and looked after him. It must have been that man's karma to be rescued; so the ones who passed by did not do him any harm. Nor did the third man do him any good which he would not have had anyway – it was his karma to be rescued.'

'That is right,' replied the teacher. 'His karma was mixed, as it nearly always is; he had done some deeds of cruelty which brought him the karma of being attacked himself; but he had also done some kindness, which saved him from dying.'

'In that case,' argued the pupil, 'there is no point in trying to do any good to people; if it is their karma to receive good, they will have it anyway; and if it is not, nothing we can do will give it to them.'

The teacher made no reply, but later on when they went for their afternoon walk, he called in at the house of a rich disciple, and came out holding a silver coin. Just outside the town he dropped this on the path, and then seated himself with the pupil a little distance away. 'It is the karma of this coin to be picked up,' he remarked, 'let us see what happens.'

Two men came walking quickly towards the town. They were quarrelling furiously. 'Why did you have to answer him back like that?' shouted one of them. 'Look at the trouble it will make for us –

# KARMA

why can't you keep *calm?* Tell yourself it takes two to make a fight.'

'It only takes one,' growled the other man, 'as you'll find out if you keep on about it . . .' and they passed, glaring at each other and without noticing the coin.

Soon afterwards came a man who was drunk; his bleary eyes could hardly make out the path, let alone the coin. He too passed by.

The next man was walking calmly. He noticed the coin, and looked around. Seeing the two, he asked, 'Have you dropped a silver coin perhaps?'

The teacher got up with marked respect and bowed as he replied. 'It does not belong to us, sir.'

The other returned the bow, and saying 'Well, I will find a use for it' went on his way.

'That one will spend it wisely' remarked the teacher appreciatively. 'But you see the point about the karma? It was its karma to be picked up, and it was picked up. But unfortunate were those who missed the opportunity, and fortunate was the one who saw it and took it. It was the same with those three men near Jerusalem; it was the victim's karma to be picked up, but fortunate was the Samaritan who actually picked him up. He was the instrument through which the blessing came, and, as the voluntary instrument of blessing, he was blessed himself.'

# UNSTEADINESS

In her last work, *Interior Castle*, St Teresa remarks that instability of
spiritual states is often a cause of bewilderment to spiritual aspirants.
They felt sure that what they experienced at times of devotion in
favourable circumstances would be with them for ever; when they
found later that somehow it had gone, they were liable to lose
confidence and give up.

A Zen master, discussing the same point, compares the spiritual
path to a journey in a rowing boat along a coast where there is a
strong tide. Half the time it helps, and half the time the tide is against
the boat. Beginners usually enter on the practice when things are
favourable, and they make rapid progress up to a point, but when
they find the 'tide' has changed, many of them become discouraged
because they find they can hardly advance any further, and they stop
trying. So the contrary tide carries them back over nearly all the
distance they covered. When it again runs for them, they make new
efforts and the spiritual qualities they had lost become manifest once
more, but when it changes, they give up as before and are carried
back, losing the spiritual intuitions and inner peace.

They can spend, he adds, a lifetime thus alternating between
elevation and depression, and never reaching the goal because they
will not row unless the current is in their favour. Even worse, some of
them may come to feel that all efforts are somehow useless, leading
only to states most of which pass away; they lose faith that there *is* any
real progress to be made.

He gives some interesting and valuable advice to disciples in this
sitation. The attainments of the favourable times, he says, are indeed
unstable, unless and until they have been held steady during an
unfavourable time. When you row with the tide, you will pass certain
points on the coast-line; but if you stop rowing when the tide turns
against you, you will be carried back past them. You will see them

# UNSTEADINESS

leaving you, so to speak. Then you will have to row past them yet again when the tide runs for you.

But if, when you have once passed them, and the contrary tide begins, you work hard to hold the boat where it is, just where it is without thinking of further progress at present, then those points are behind you for ever. Never again will you have to struggle past them.

If you attain a state of some peace in peaceful surroundings, you do not know whether that state will remain with you or not. But if you have managed even once to retain some degree of it during a time of serious disturbance, then that degree of peace is yours for ever. And the same with other spiritual qualities. This is the advice of Zen Master Hakuin.

# THE NESTING INSTINCT

It was an old country, hundreds of years behind the times, and a small group of young people in the capital began agitating for reform. They themselves lived on little, and spent their time finding out the vested interests and centres of inertia that kept their country backward, and exposing them in little duplicated leaflets. An important factor in their growing success was the examples they cited of other countries which had successfully reformed. Others began to join them.

The Home Minister sent a private message to them, 'I am a supporter of your ideas, but cannot declare myself for you publicly; I can help you better by remaining at my post. But I can arrange for the transfer to you of a house with a considerable estate and several cottages; it is a bit outside the capital and rather tumble-down, but you could get it straight and then have a proper centre. Moreover there is an old disused printing press in the basement which you could repair and get going, and there are big stocks of old numbers of foreign magazines, which would help you with your propaganda. The price would be merely nominal.'

The group discussed it and joyfully agreed. They moved in, and found that the place was indeed tumble-down and neglected. However they worked hard to make a couple of cottages livable, and to make the main house an administrative centre where they could also study the literature; two of them began to learn the foreign languages in which it was mainly written. The printing press was a problem, but they gradually came to understand it and began to search for spare parts for this old model.

In the capital less was heard of their movement, but the Cabinet came to know of their new centre, and were worried what would happen when they got it organized. 'How did they get hold of such a place?' The Home Minister reassured them: '*I* arranged for them to have it.'

# THE NESTING INSTINCT

'Are you mad? It will be a splendid centre for them; previously they had nothing. Once they get it going . . .'

'Don't worry,' he said, 'they will never get it going. They have to work hard to keep up the place, and they are improving the gardens now. Some of them have taken jobs to get money to pay for the materials. Those two will take years to learn the foreign languages, and it will take a life-time to get the printing press going, because spare parts for that old model are no longer made. They still mouth their slogans, but the means have become the end; they are marrying and settling in the rent-free cottages. The nesting instinct has taken over.'

# NEW

A new disciple joined the group, who did not seem to have the usual set of virtues and vices. He somehow managed to be both arrogant and cringing, over-blunt and hypocritical, lazy and yet fussy over trivialities, timid and then suddenly reckless.

The head disciple remarked to the teacher, 'I don't know how we are going to make anything out of him.'

That evening the teacher was taking his evening walk with the head disciple and two others, and the teacher prolonged the walk till late into the night. Finally they returned by way of the house of a famous university professor, known for his aggressiveness and irascibility, and who was also a heavy drinker. He had just published a book on some intricate points in the philosophy of Chandrakirti.

It was a hot summer evening, and they saw that the professor, as usual in the summer, had his bed on the verandah. He was asleep, breathing heavily, but muttering in his dreams. 'Listen,' said the teacher softly, 'what is he saying?' They held their breath and listened, but it was only disjointed words and nonsensical phrases, mixed up with the name Chandrakirti and some technical philosophical terms.

'Why,' said the teacher to the head disciple, 'he is talking absolute nonsense. You could easily expose his errors – you were saying the other day that you doubted that he was always right.'

Then he called loudly, 'Professor, professor! My disciple here wants to debate with you on Chandrakirti.'

The professor rolled over and sat up unsteadily, feeling for his slippers. 'Whassat? . . . I'll debate him!' and he shouted for some coffee to the sleeping household.

But the disciple had fled.

Next day the teacher said to him: 'You didn't wait for the professor, though he was talking quite idiotically, because you knew that within him was the famous scholar, just over-shadowed for the moment. You weren't simple-minded enough to think that those ravings of his were his real nature. What you said about the new disciple was too simple-minded. When he sits down to meditate, there is a god in full splendour meditating there. His problem is to realize it, and we shall help him to do that. It is not a question of making anything out of him.'

# LOOKING UP

A small undeveloped country discovered some mineral resources, and the enlightened government decided on a policy of rapid change to universal literacy and education. An enterprising education minister sent a number of idealistic students to train abroad as teachers; when they returned he despatched them to small towns and villages.

'The main thing,' he told them, 'is to show the country people that they can do it; then we can bring out every scrap of the undiscovered ability in our people. In addition to getting the school going, I want you to develop gradually a highest class of promising boys and girls of seventeen. In five years time, I shall come round and will arrange for two or three of the best from each school to be given free education at the university in the capital, plus a later stay abroad if they do well. In twenty years we shall transform the country. As you perhaps know, there was opposition to sending you abroad; people said that we needed the able ones at home. You too will be criticized, but I want you to persist. Don't be diverted from what you are doing.'

His vision caught fire in them, and full of enthusiasm they went out. After the five years, one such teacher duly received an official letter saying that the minister was coming to inspect his school. It was accompanied by a personal note from the minister himself, saying, 'I hear you have been working hard, and I have been working too. Our plan will go ahead, and I look forward to seeing you and your school.'

When the minister arrived they greeted each other warmly. The elder man looked over the school and said he was very satisfied: 'This bears out the reports I have had from the inspectors. Now show me your special class. I take it they are all keen to go?' 'Oh yes', said the teacher, 'it is the heart's desire of all the village youngsters.'

They went to a classroom where there were about twenty boys and girls. The minister seated himself at the teacher's table on the little dais, introduced himself, and looked for a moment at each one. Then he said,

'You know that the government which I serve sometimes arranges for students like you to go to the university in the capital, and perhaps later abroad for a year or so. There is no competitive examination for these chances, though of course we do take your school record into account. Perhaps from one school half a dozen might be invited, and perhaps none. We have our own method of selection – but you all have a chance.

'Now having said that, I want you each to imagine that you individually have been chosen. You can go and study anything you like. Afterwards you may be able to go on to a foreign country where there is specialized advanced training in your favourite subject. Now write me a paper explaining what you would like to do, and why. You have an hour to do it.'

As they bent their heads to begin, he said to the teacher, 'I want to see their exercise books on composition and also mathematics.' The teacher got the books and held them in a pile, ready to pass them one by one to the minister, but the latter took two or three and opened them flat on the table. He seemed to be comparing them. Then he said shortly, 'Just put them in a pile here on the side of the table.' He took more and more off, laying them open side by side, and pushing the pile to make room. Finally he gave one push too many and they all crashed to the floor.

The teacher picked them up, but the minister now seemed to have lost interest. He sat on the edge of the table and began to tell a slightly scandalous story about a newspaper editor who had been castigating in his paper opium smoking and other offences which he himself was committing in private.

Somehow the hour passed, and the children handed in their essays and departed. The minister did not examine them carefully: he did

# LOOKING UP

not even look at them. The young schoolmaster was almost in tears as he realized that his patron, who he had respected and even revered, was becoming senile. As he looked sadly at the floor, the minister remarked briskly, 'It's those two, isn't it? The girl at the back with her hair done up in that big knot, and the boy in the second row, at the right-hand end. Those are the two we want. What are their names?'

The teacher gaped. 'How did you know? Those are the best two, though there is another one who's very clever – the fat boy.'

'Oh no, not him,' said the minister. 'When I pushed those books over, he looked up, just like all the others except those two. And when I was telling that story, he had an occasional peep at me. Those two were the only ones who weren't diverted by me.

'The others, however clever they might be, when they got to the big city and still more if they got abroad, would look up. And then their studies would go to pieces. Our country is at a parting of the ways, and we want students who will not look up.

'I asked them to write about their heart's desire. We want people who don't look up when it is a question of their heart's desire.'